A Life Well Lived

David James Crellin

1962 - 2017

His life in our words and pictures

In the months following David's untimely death there was a huge outpouring of emotion, the practical outcome of which was a collection of photographs and memories which I just couldn't let go to waste. Putting together this collection has been a work of remembrance, healing and pride. It has also been, in David's best tradition, A Project. David touched so many people's lives. I have learned a lot of things I previously didn't know about him, and so I imagine will anyone reading through this collection.

Thank you to everyone who has helped me put names and dates to photographs. I can't guarantee everything is correct, but we have done our best! Where I have taken a liberty with a quote, for clarity or any other reason, I apologise.

Proceeds from the sale of this book are donated to cancer research.

It has been my privilege to know David for the whole of his life, and to put together this tribute to a life well lived.

(Half Uncle) Frank Boddy

First published 2019.

Edited by Frank Boddy.
Image and text copyrights belong to the individual authors and contributors.
Permission to reproduce the poem *David's Ashes* is given by Barbara Rigg.
The opinions expressed in this work are those of individual contributors.

A catalogue record for this book is available from the British Library.

ISBN: 978-1-911526-30-8

Publisher:
Milton Contact Ltd.
3, Hall End, Milton, Cambridge, CB24 6AQ, UK
www.miltoncontact.co.uk

EARLY YEARS

I have watched Dave grow
from a baby into a man of
whom I am very proud.

Barbara Crellin

*Baby David
1962*

*With Albert the rabbit, at Holly
Gate Road
1963*

*John, Half Uncle Frank and
David in the sand boat, St Bees
c. 1966*

To say I was slightly in awe of Dave was an understatement! He always seemed so confident, organised and in charge!

Rachel Crellin

I remember Boxing day parties at Hollygate Road. Great times.

Tim Pollitt

*At Holly Gate Road, Dalton
c. 1967*

Dave hasn't always been the methodical, logical, organised thorough individual that we know and love. In fact as a child he was just bloody difficult.

Frank Boddy

With cousins Sue and Steve Crellin
c. 1966

I am so proud and lucky to have him as a cousin.

Sue Crellin

At Undergreens Road, Barrow
c. 1966

My earliest memories of David were as a toddler at Undergreens Road, before [the Crellins] moved as a family to the Wirral.

John Boddy

I first met David at primary school when we were seven and he has been an important part of my life ever since.

Bill Rigg

Picnic with (Mum) Carol Crellin and cousin Steve Crellin
c. 1964

My Mum thought he was great: dependable, reliable and trustworthy in short, a very good role model for me!

Brian Acott

With cousins Steve and Sue Crellin
c. 1964

Cousins Sue and Steve Crellin, and David holding chubby little brother John c. 1966

David, John and Frank on the beach c. 1971

Chris and I played a board game with David – something incredibly complex like snakes and ladders, or ludo, and Chris happened to win. Well, tears welled up in David's eyes, his lower lip started to tremble, and he spluttered out the words "But I have to win!!"

John Boddy

My memories of him are forever inextricably linked with times of great happiness and celebration - parties, weekends and New Year's away in the Lakes, Dales or Moors, weddings and in general opportunities to relax, have fun and chat over one of our mutual loves - a few pints of good ale!

Richard Noble

School photo
c. 1969

Johns, David and Frank on a picnic in front of Grandpa Boddy's Morris Oxford c. 1971

*Uncle Dan Crellin, brother John,
cousin Steve
c. 1970*

Dave leads me off for a walk in the dunes and proceeds to introduce me to the concept of snogging! An education and enlightenment on what it actually was and then how to do it!

Sue Crellin

*L to R: Andy Riding, Rachel,
Chris Riding, John, Steve, Sue,
David
c. 1969*

Dave was my "big cousin" and I was the baby of the family.

Rachel Crellin

TEENAGE & UNIVERSITY

We listened to Super Tramp on the cassette player and gazed out through the moonlight down the valley to the sea and up to the stars, bonding with the Universe with the assistance of some special hand rolled herbal cigarettes which David had procured

Brian Acott

Family gathering at Stonestar: Jason, Richard, Cathy, John, Alex (was Sandy then), David, Andy, Frank
c. 1981

David, Magnum aka John, Carol and Uncle Dan
c. 1987

The Crellin Family
c. 1987

Car posing
c. 1981

Well, Dave was driving not exactly slowly and I still don't know if he simply hadn't seen the humpback bridge, but when we parted contact with the road, three heads (in these pre-seatbelt law days) simultaneously hit the underside of the car roof before milliseconds later our three coccyxes became permanently compressed as we landed.

Alex Boddy

He pulled up in the dark on the grass verge outside the cottage and it was later discovered had run over the neighbour's prize rose bush in the process. This resulted in Frank and I being blacklisted from ever using the cottage again

Margaret Boddy

Early Dave-mobile at Stonestar c. 1980

I was very jealous of his Golf GTI but he left the keys in the ignition when he nipped into the kiosk in a petrol station and somebody drove it away with all his caving and walking gear in it.

Craig Oliver

The (in)famous Golf GTI c. 1986

Concentrating on driving (for once)
c. 1980

Between beers and getting me into Steely Dan and Tangerine Dream he did show me parts of the university

Alex Boddy

Denim and Yellow Chevette
c. 1980

Dave was steadfast in his views. Stubborn might be another way of saying it. I remember the three of us arguing with Dave that his shaving in the bath was leaving stubble embedded in the scum around the bath. Goes without saying that the scum was acceptable to us students, but not his stubble.

Colin Bowes

There were other wild moments... the Hawk Lords concert incident, when he dived out of the top floor window during the Great Storm of 1987...

Bill Rigg

Fresh faced
c.1983

Dave refused to lock the door when taking a bath, in case someone else wanted to use the facilities.

Tony Liddar

On the train heading for a
walking trip with Craig
1983

New Year at Coniston
1992

We both moved into the same student flat (Lupton) in Leeds, in September 1981 and he was immediately the ring leader in marshalling the 5 of us new friends straight out on a pub crawl

Craig Oliver

New Year in the cottage at Coniston
1992

He re-emerged in the adjacent [paternoster] shaft heading downwards, having (while out-of-sight) completely inverted himself within the lift.

Alex Boddy

Early beard attempt
c. 1982

At Leeds Uni
Bill Rigg as Begbie, years before
Trainspotting came out
c. 1980

CHARLOTTE & DAVID

Dave's 40th, Archway House
2002

Charlotte introduces David to Claire as "The only man you'll ever meet who stock rotates his socks."

Claire & James Smith

New Year at Coniston
1992

Those Manchester days when he met Charlotte through my sister, Charlotte, who shared a flat with her just up the road

Anne Jury

Charlotte, Charlie and Ollie...the three of you were everything to David

John Crellin

*A special present
c. 1990*

Love doesn't go away. David will always be a part of us – and we have that to treasure always

Sue Crellin

*Another special present
c. 1990*

*Simon, Fiona, Naughty Norm,
David & Charlotte,
Stonestar
1994*

Wedding guests
c.1992

It was evident early on, once he met Charlotte, that he'd found the person who fulfilled him

Margaret Boddy

New Year at Coniston
1992

Charlotte reminds me that when he first took her out I gave her a lecture about not messing him about, well she never did

Charlotte Mouncey

Ann & Stewart's wedding 1999

I recall advising him to go out with the (a lot younger) Charlotte. Good advice, as it turns out

Tony Liddar

River tour, London 2008

18th December, 1993

FAMILY

David (and you [John]) cared for Carol and Norman with such devotion during their respective illnesses What struck me was David's acceptance of the situation, and his calmness, coupled with strong determination to ensure that that their final years (particularly in Carol's case) were as comfortable as possible.

John Boddy

The koi pond, Loxley Road 2002

At the seaside c. 2004

Macclesfield Canal
2003

I feel sure that he will have left everything in good order. Always very proud of you and Charlie and Ollie.

Nicholas Frobisher

Charlotte, Ollie, David and Charlie
2003

I remember being moved
by the beautiful letters
which he and you wrote
to Dora after my father
had died, and thinking at
the time that there were
not many grandchildren
who would find the words
to express their feelings in
the way that you did.

John Boddy

*At the seaside
c. 2003*

Brittany
c. 2004

Chris and I will remember him as a thoroughly decent man, always putting others first

John Boddy

Talylln Railway
c. 2004

I automatically looked up to him. However, even within his peer group he always projected an air of calm, intelligent authority and resourcefulness.

Brian Acott

I am so pleased that he was able to attend mine and Rebecca's wedding last year and that my final contact with him was at such a happy occasion.

Brian Acott

With Charlie, Ollie and Norm
c. 2004

Crich campers
2009

Trevi Fountain
2007

Barcelona
2012

The lovely home that David and Charlotte made together to share with Charlie and Ollie bears testament to his graft and his desire to create a haven for his family

John Crellin

I remember him being immediately helpful, charming in a quiet way, straightforward and definitely on top of the logistics.

Margaret Boddy

Oslo
2008

Pride Park
2009

There was a particularly energetic attempt at goal from Simon which resulted in the ball shattering one of the windows in David's much-loved shed. David gave a very muted response in the circumstances

Margaret Boddy

Barcelona
c. 2012

Even in his final months there was never a suggestion that he was suffering any injustice or unfairness; all he said was... he was just a bit disappointed with the way things had worked out. That was David.

John Crellin

Crich campers
2009

Family Portrait
c. 2009

BROTHERS

It's high time I shut up because I'm wasting V.D.T. - Valuable Drinking Time – and we don't want that fine for over-running our time slot.

John Crellin

Cousin Cathy's 21st birthday party

Boating at Todmorden 1999

The way he managed to
sneak in a motorbike after
he'd turned 50 helps us
remember that for him, it
was always about living
life to the full.

John Crellin

*Christmas
c. 2000*

*In the pub
c. 1995*

Happily at the tiller
c. 2008

My big brother...my hero...

David, wish you were here.

John Crellin

BEER

So many of my times with
David have involved beer;
I'll never drink another
pint without thinking
about him.

Craig Oliver

*The Power of Beer, with Kevin
Ellis and James Smith
2015*

That wonderful
"aaaaahhhh" he would
utter as he sank the first
draught of his first pint in
some lunchtime canal
side pub with the sun
streaming in through the
window will always stay
with me.

Frank Boddy

Tasting Session with John, Norm, and Dan
c. 1982

David asked how long until dinner, "30 minutes", said Deborah; then came the look at me, the gesture towards to pub next door and a swift half (3 pints) in the 30 minute interval.

Craig Oliver

Barcelona
2012

The Thursday before the Saturday of the crawl, Dave went round each pub on his bike and had a half pint just to make sure that the beer on his watch was as good as it could be

Alex Boddy

BOATING

David's skippering on the
canal boat trips is now
legendary

Margaret Boddy

*Four Counties Ring
Debbie, Margaret, Ros, Deborah,
John, David,
Craig, Frank
1987*

*Four Counties Ring, with Ros
1987*

Four Counties Ring, with Deborah

Narrow boating was another of David's passions and eight of us managed a long weekend on a canal or river every year, something we all looked forward to almost from the moment we'd completed the previous trip.

John Crellin

On The River Barrow, Ireland 1989

He never shied away from telling me something I might not want to hear.

Craig Oliver

*Four Counties Ring: John, Margaret,
Frank, David
1987*

The River Barrow, Ireland, with Craig

The River Barrow, Ireland, with Roger

I don't think I ever saw or heard David judge anyone. I think he simply slotted it into a memory bank as another person that Nature had created.

Rob England

Hauling the boat in, with Bill Rigg

He wished all of us well in life, and when we saw each other, we just carried on where we left off. And when we parted company, he wished us well wherever the journey took us

Rob England

IN THE KITCHEN AT PARTIES

Whenever David visited us the kitchen would be guaranteed to end up cleaner than it had been before he arrived

Margaret Boddy

Cooking a full boating breakfast 2008

Any party of ours that Dave came to, he was always first up, bin liners in hand and had cleared up and had tea in the pot before anyone else had even opened an eye!

Sue Crellin

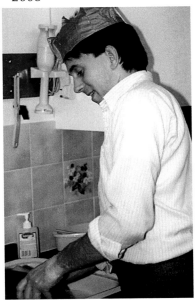

Christmas at Stonestar c. 1991

Osmotherly
c. 1980

I remember him in Leeds consuming a mashed potato sandwich to ensure that it didn't go to waste!

Jon Wray

Osmotherly
c. 1998

The cafetière was never cleaner than after a Crellin stay - David always dismantled the whole thing and cleaned the filter and screwed it all back together

Jane Wray

[My Mum] loved the way when he stayed at my parents' house, at dinner he would ask for a spoon to eat all the gravy, then devour her sticky toffee pudding and ask for more, and then he would stand up and say "right, I'll do the washing up"

Craig Oliver

Christmas at Stonestar
c. 2000

OUTDOOR LIFE

*Resting in thought
c. 1987*

*Four Counties Ring
1987*

We climbed up high early on and stayed on the tops all day, doing many peaks. By the time evening came, we started dropping down and I thought I'd really earned a few beers, until David looked at a peak to our left and said "Ooh! We haven't done that one!" Which we did. Ouch.

Claire & James Smith

I enjoyed some of the best Lake District walking with Dave and Bill over those Manchester years.

Anne Jury

Walking trip with Craig 1983

David had a real calculated calmness in any risk situation (that's bravery isn't it?), self-effacing humour and sense of the absurd

Craig Oliver

Posing on the Cumberland Way 1990

*Coniston Old Man
c. 1985*

The worse the weather, the more Dave enjoyed going for a walk up a mountain. I think the philosophy was that the nastier it was outside, the nicer it was when you got back to the pub

Anne Jury

*Coast to Coast Walk, with Bill
Rigg
1988*

Shorts - as soon as the sun was out and over 10 degrees – Shorts

Nick Rowson-Jones

*Coast to Coast Walk
1988*

*Crib Goch, Snowden
2010*

Appleby Station, Cumberland Way 1990

Woe betide anybody that dare criticise his meticulous planning or attempt to wrestle the map off him

John Crellin

Cumberland Way: John, David and Carol 1990

First he did one of his favourite tricks and shouted "Whoa!"........frantic stabbing of brakes from Craig ...pause "I'm going' to Barbados....Whoa in de sunny Caribbean Sea";

Craig Oliver

Being sensible, I did what
you are meant to do,
which is to walk around
the perimeter of the
field so that you are
always a few yards from a
fence you can hop over.
But not David. He walked
across the middle and
right past the bull, talking
to the animal loudly

Craig Oliver

*Cumberland Way route
planning:
David and Carol
1990*

*Ravenglass, Carol, John and
David
1990*

Ostel Bay, Argyll, with Jon Wray
c. 1990

Ollie, Charlie, Charlotte, Carol, David
c. 2005

Whilst we were having our picnic I managed to sneak two large rocks in to the bottom of his rucksack. It was not until we stopped 2 or 3 miles later when David reached in to find something that he discovered them. I'll never forget the look of disbelief on his face that he "super organized logistics Dave "had failed to notice the additional weight!

Jon Wray

I think he'd miscalculated the effect his leap would have on the canoe and he floated off away from the river bank leaving him stranded without a paddle.

Dom Andrews

Family boating
c. 2005

Punctures, bad weather or fatigue were usually met with a mixture of stoic patience, good-natured teasing and a considerate open-ness that made his company a joy.

Dom Andrews

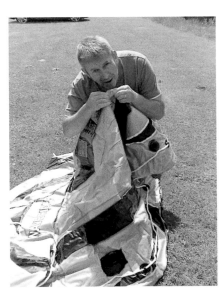

Crich Campers
2009

*Men Overboard, with Charlie
and Ollie
2009*

*Isle of Bute, with Charlotte,
Charlie and Ollie
2003*

We worked, talked, hugged, kissed, drank, fixed things, walked, solved problems and explored ideas honestly together where ever and whenever we were together, True friends they say a man can count on one hand, I am proud to call David my friend, he will never ever be forgotten.

Tom McCarthy

David proceeded to ascertain whether silver birch was the best fire lighter there and then in the middle of the gardens! It was then established that it was a good idea to carry this particular bark in ones pocket for emergencies!

Jane Wray

*Isle of Bute, with Charlotte
2003*

I recall with great affection his habit of stimulating a good debate in the pub by throwing a topic out there we could all latch onto. I will miss his gentle spirit, strong values and his very warm welcome whenever I joined the crew in the pub.

Mark Judd

*Isle of Bute
2003*

David was both tactile and loving. I guess this was just a constituent part of his wearing of his heart on his sleeve, but this did make him quite unique among men

Alex Boddy

*Crich Wheelers
2006*

Outside their house, on the street with some of his little pals, they were all on bikes, and it was apparent to me that Dave was the 'boss'

Sue Crellin

Dave had an infectious gurgling laugh – just like you!
He also had a classic "Ministry of Funny Walks" way of walking – lurching ahead with large strides and leaning forward

Tony Liddar

Crich Wheelers
2006

FIXIT / PLAN IT

Italy
2010

Dave was completely calm, collected and enthusiastically putting his all into the job – no signs of impatience, or annoyance at having lost days of holiday to such a task, and seemingly enjoying the logistical challenge!

Sue Crellin

Crich Campers
2009

David loved a project.

John Crellin

David [left] sitting amongst his camping possessions after realising he had forgotten to bring his tent.

Mark Judd

*Crich Campers
2009*

Retirement for David might well have involved many hours in his shed crafting the next project.

John Crellin

*Crich Campers
2009*

Crich Wheelers
2006

There was nobody better than David to have by your side in a crisis. How many times in my life – in many of our lives – have we said to ourselves "How would David do this?"

John Crellin

Walking trip with Craig
1983

Not only did he patiently hang mirrors, pictures, curtain poles and make fabulous doors for Madame Beaumont... in the Beaumont house he was always fondly known as "fix-it"

Rachel Beaumont

Logs - I still can't believe I have had conversations regarding the orientation and rotation of log piles for hours

Nick Rowson-Jones

Dave, Tom and the boys (theirs and ours) would set off with Machetes, saws, strimmers and other tools in hand to complete a project that would contribute to the forest's welfare in some shape or form.

Sue Crellin

In the workshop with Charlie c.2006

Crich Wheelers
2006

The most unique thing is his voice, which I can still clearly hear in my head: a mixture of Nanna Crellin (originator of the phrase 'Our David'), Norman, a certain grainy whine and always a slight tetchy indication that he wasn't completely happy with the way everyone was doing everything

Frank Boddy

Crich Campers
2009

Only last week I was trying to drill a hole in a piece of wood with a masonry bit and said out loud "David wouldn't do this" and went and bought a proper set of drill bits.

Bill Rigg

FESTIVALS

"Character-building" and "Earning your pleasure" were phrases that David would often use.

John Crellin

*Cropredy
2010*

Bearded Theory
2012

FMS – the medical charity that David and I volunteered for – asked yesterday if they can plant a tree at the Glastonbury Festival site in dedication to David

John Crellin

Bearded Theory. With Dom
2014

He was completely non-judgmental, and looked at every situation practically. Things were what they were with Dave – no prejudice coloured his point of view – as has been said about him, it just went into his data bank of things, types of people, situations, problems, challenges to be experienced.

Sue Crellin

Dave told me that he had been listening to Steve (Hewlett)'s chats about his cancer with Eddie Mair on Radio 4 months before he too was diagnosed with exactly the same cancer.

Rachel Crellin

Glastonbury, South East Corner Incident
2013

Glastonbury
2016

CHARACTER

An interesting look
c. 1980

Dave's life was Quality, and was all about Quality.

Frank Boddy

His sock drawer was always a marvel to me, his pencil & pen box a wonder and his shed and garage something I could only dream of.

Bill Rigg

Life is just too short; we will remember him and make sure every minute counts as he would have wanted

Nicholas Frobisher

c. 2003

David was an exceptional person; he was confident and clever without any trace of ego or arrogance. He was thoughtful and considerate and never selfish. He was in every way, a better man than I.

Bill Rigg

c. 2005

c. 2005

No-one but Dave could have made stylish the wearing of a black donkey jacket with the letters NCB decorating the orange reflective strip running across the upper back

Alex Boddy

Inverary Jail
c. 2006

His was a life well lived and - although so sadly far too short - was full of love and happy times.

Rachel Crellin

He was a great person who was great to be around

Fred Smith

Deborah & Craig's wedding c. 1989

We joked about him lying on his cv that he played sports on a regular basis, although he had never done anything – ever! He thought that watching his beloved Barrow counted in this regard

Tony Liddar

c. 1997

c. 1980

He is the most honest and principled person I have ever known.

Bill Rigg

Robin Hoods Bay
c. 2010

I smuggled him onto a secure Ministry of Defence site hidden in the boot of my car.

Bill Rigg

That he had taken the time to send [his notes on my programme] and to really think about them was so kind and supportive - and I was that little girl again - beaming with pride - in awe of my" big cousin" who had thought something I had done was ok!

Rachel Crellin

c. 2004

May it prompt us to reach out more often, love each harder, and treasure the persistent threads of web-like connection which Dave built in life.

Helen Parker

*Norfolk
2005*

71

He never seemed to let anything ruffle him – his unbelievable patience and forbearance with his Mother in Law is the best case in point

Claire & James Smith

Barcelona
c. 2012

I was never deemed worthy enough to see the drawer myself, but I have adopted one of its features. That of the "Hopeful section", where long lost socks were allowed to linger in the hope that one day they might be reunited with their partner.

Andrew Briggs

Norfolk
2005

The noise he made when tasting something really good, & sharing a bottle or few of red wine, a log fire & some prog rock till the early hours.

Ian Lawrence

c. 2006

One of the things I will miss and always think of with David is the great bear hug he would give.

Margaret Boddy

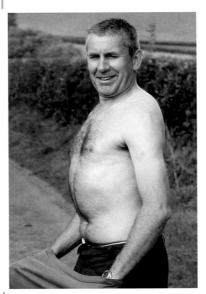

Crich Wheelers
c. 2006

David's Ashes

David though you're gone away from us,
You're organised, as usual to the last.
A night of heavy rain ensured the river was in spate
With sunny day to follow tempering the sadness of the cast,
All this from on high.

Before you went, the scene was carefully planned,
The bridge at Cockley Beck providing an ideal
Place for your send-off down the stream.
All with a dry and stable place to stand.
As you flew through the air.

The peat-brown water carrying you past old haunts.
Birk's Bridge, with clear, deep pool,
Ideal for jumping in.
Fickle Steps and the Gorge beyond
Where many a walk has ended,
Before Arrival at Newfield and the cheer within,
A beer and wholesome fare.

Watersmeet comes next,
An easy place to bathe, well known.
Before the trundle down to Seathwaite Bridge.
Where the ancient petrol pumps once stood
And the outline of a salmon, carved in stone,
A champion caught.

The next bridge down is Ulpha,
Making a dog-leg of the road.

Where picnickers encamp in summer and young boys
Plummet from the rampart into the clear, deep water
As it glides beneath, without a noise.
A daring sport.

Then at last you reach your favourite place
Stone Star pool, what happy times you had there,
Playing in the water with inflated boats and balls.
Friends, family and dogs were everywhere
As we lay next the pool.

After this excitement you slow down
To go beneath Rawfold
Passing Duddon Hall, where in the Springs
The daffodils delight us from among the trees.
Then the pebble beach where you played of old.
Paddling after school.

In later years the Sheep Dip was the place for bathing
Stepping on large boulders between fish and weed.
Then lying on the old wharf in the sun to dry
And eat a picnic, or just laze and read.
You felt grown-up then,

And so the passage of the river reflects life and death
A catalogue of memories, a potent legacy
Of events, from early childhood and to middle age.
The Duddon sees it all as it flows towards the sea
And the far beyond

Barbara Rigg

Valedictory Sonnet to The River Duddon

I THOUGHT of Thee, my partner and my guide,
 As being pass'd away.--Vain sympathies!
 For, backward, Duddon! as I cast my eyes,
I see what was, and is, and will abide;
Still glides the Stream, and shall for ever glide;
 The Form remains, the Function never dies;
 While we, the brave, the mighty, and the wise,
We Men, who in our morn of youth defied
The elements, must vanish;--be it so!
 Enough, if something from our hands have power
 To live, and act, and serve the future hour;
And if, as toward the silent tomb we go,
 Through love, through hope, and faith's transcendent dower,
We feel that we are greater than we know.

William Wordsworth

> *The ashes of Ann Carol Crellin and Norman Crellin
> are scattered at Duddon Pool; and those of David
> James Crellin at Cockley Beck, towards the river's
> upper reaches.*